BARBARA ADAMS AND KRZYSZTOF M. CIAŁOWICZ

PROTODYNASTIC EGYPT

Cover photograph
Monumental limestone statue of the ithyphallic god Min from the temple at Koptos. (Ash. 1894.105e, courtesy of the Visitors of the Ashmolean Museum, Oxford.)

British Library Cataloguing in Publication Data:
Adams, Barbara, 1945-
Protodynastic Egypt. – (Shire Egyptology; 25)
1. Egypt – History – To 332 B. C.
2. Egypt – Civilization – To 332 B. C.
I. Title II. Cialowicz, Krzysztof M.
932'. 012
ISBN 0 7478 0357 9

Published by
SHIRE PUBLICATIONS LTD
Cromwell House, Church Street, Princes Risborough,
Buckinghamshire HP27 9AA, UK.

Series Editor: Barbara Adams

ISBN 0 7478 0357 9.

First published 1997.

Printed in Great Britain by
CIT Printing Services, Press Buildings,
Merlins Bridge, Haverfordwest, Pembrokeshire SA61 1XF.

Contents

Acknowledgements

Despite being separated by the breadth of Europe and meeting only occasionally, it has been a pleasure for the authors to collaborate with little disagreement on a subject which invokes such varied opinion. Supportive colleagues who helped with the provision of illustrations are Helen Whitehouse, Karla Kroeper, Renée Friedman, Günter Dreyer, David Rice and Stan Hendrickx. Figures 10, 15, 18, 21, 31, 33 and 44 are the work of Helena Jaeschke, and figures 23-30 and 38-40 are by Krzysztof M. Ciałowicz.

4

List of illustrations

Chronology

Based on W. J. Murnane, *The Penguin Guide to Ancient Egypt*, 1983.

Palaeolithic   500,000-5500 BC

Predynastic	5500-3050 BC	
Early Predynastic	5500-3800 BC	Fayum A, Merimda, Badarian
	3800-3500 BC	Amratian (Naqada IA-IB)
Middle Predynastic	3550-3400 BC	Early Gerzean (Naqada IC, IIA-B)
Late Predynastic	3400-3300 BC	Middle Gerzean (Naqada IIC)
	3300-3200 BC	Late Gerzean (Naqada IID1-IID2)
Protodynastic	3200-3050 BC	(Naqada IIIA1-IIIC1)

Early Dynastic	3050-2613 BC	
	3050-2890 BC	Dynasty I (Naqada IIIC1-IIID)
	2890-2686 BC	Dynasty II (Naqada IIID)

Old Kingdom   2686-2181 BC   Dynasties III-VI

First Intermediate Period
     2181-2040 BC   Dynasties VII-XI (1)

Middle Kingdom   2040-1782 BC   Dynasties XI (2)-XII

Second Intermediate Period
     1782-1570 BC   Dynasties XIII-XVII

New Kingdom   1570-1070 BC   Dynasties XVIII-XX

Third Intermediate Period
     1070-713 BC   Dynasties XXI-XXIV

Late Period   713-332 BC   Dynasties XXV-XXXI

Graeco-Roman Period
     332 BC-AD 395   Ptolemies and Roman Emperors

1

The Late Predynastic scene

In Egypt the bridge between prehistory and history was a short but crucial period of transition when the nation formed into a united state ruled by one king. Although there was cultural continuity and the period was profoundly affected by the cultural expansion which had taken place in the Gerzean (Naqada II) and the preceding Amratian (Naqada I) phases of the Predynastic, there was enough dynamic change to warrant its definition here as the Protodynastic (Naqada III). There is constant controversy concerning the period and the processes by which transformation came about, and this is enlivened whenever a new discovery is made.

The chronological framework is basically the same relative scheme that is used for the Predynastic period, based on the seriation of grave goods, chiefly pottery. It was devised by William Matthew Flinders Petrie at the beginning of the twentieth century and refined by Werner Kaiser in the 1950s. The system has been adjusted by taking into account a suite of radiocarbon dates and the appearance of writing and commemorative objects with important scenes. In the last quarter of the twentieth century renewed excavation in Upper and Lower Egypt has produced a range of new data and prompted scholars, such as Stan Hendrickx, to rework the seriation by analysing spatial distribution in the cemeteries. There is some difference in detail but most researchers accept that Naqada III can be subdivided and that Naqada IIIc, sometimes called 'Dynasty 0', is the last phase before the unification of Egypt. This phase definitely includes the named king of Upper Egypt, Narmer, and some Egyptologists identify named kings preceding him in Naqada IIIb-IIIc.

Relative dating has assumed renewed importance because recent carbon-14 dates for this short period are two hundred years or more too old compared with the Gerzean and Protodynastic relative dates at the pivotal sites of Hierakonpolis and Abydos. This may be due to the arrested growth of plant materials used for analysis which stopped taking in carbon-14 during drought conditions about 3500-3400 BC and then remained dormant before rainy conditions returned and the stems and branches were harvested for use in construction.

Fascination with the mysteries of Egyptian history is not unique to the present day. Even in the later periods of ancient history both the Egyptians and citizens of the Graeco-Roman world were unable to separate legend from reality. Mythologised stories appeared, presenting a specific mixture of fact and invention, from which it is difficult to pick out the seeds of truth.

The most important of the ancient Egyptian historical sources are:

1. The Royal Annals, known as the Palermo Stone, executed in the Fifth Dynasty, and containing a list of rulers in chronological order. Fragments of the inscription are preserved in the museums of Palermo and Cairo and in the Petrie Museum of Egyptian Archaeology in London.

2. The King-List of Abydos, inscribed in a corridor in the temple of Seti I, and containing a selection of the names of pharaohs until his reign in the Nineteenth Dynasty (1291-1278 BC).

3. The Turin Canon, a papyrus in Turin Museum, with a full list of kings recorded in the New Kingdom. Unfortunately it was badly damaged by careless handling and its reconstruction is controversial.

The history of Egypt was also described in the records of ancient historians and travellers who wrote in Greek and Latin. The most important of these writings are:

1. The history of Egypt, preserved in fragments, which was written by Manetho, a priest living in the third century BC.

2. A fifth-century BC record by Herodotus, the Greek 'Father of Modern History'.

The documents indicate that before the beginning of the First Dynasty Egypt was divided into two kingdoms: the northern state with its capital in Buto (Pe and Dep); and the southern one, whose capital was Hierakonpolis (Nekhen). The rulers of these kingdoms were described as the 'Followers of Horus'. Legend invested them with semi-divine, semi-human nature, making them heroes said to have reigned in the prehistoric period. According to the Turin Canon and the King-List of Abydos, the unifier of the state and the first ruler of the First Dynasty bore the name of Meni, identified by Herodotus with Men (Min) and by Manetho with Menes. King Menes was said to have laid the foundations of the later development of the united kingdom and to have established its new capital, the white-walled city of Memphis, which is near present-day Cairo.

The ancient records have been cross-linked with the results of the archaeological excavations begun in the late nineteenth century to form the foundation of numerous modern theories concerning the genesis of the kingdom on the Nile. At the beginning of the twentieth century Petrie saw the formation of the Egyptian nation as the effect of an invasion from Sumer and Elam by the 'Dynastic Race' believed to have founded the First Dynasty. According to another theory espoused by Kurt Sethe and James Breasted a few years later, Upper Egypt was conquered by the inhabitants of the Delta in the period of

1. A new interpretation by Krzysztof M. Ciałowicz of the Scorpion mace-head from the Main Deposit in the temple of Nekhen, Hierakonpolis. (Ash. E.3632.)

transition from Naqada I to Naqada II, intimating that the beginning of the latter culture should be sought in that then unexplored region. Later on, towards the end of the Naqada II phase, the south was said to have shaken off the yoke of the north. The third hypothesis, prevalent among Egyptologists until recent years, refuted prior Lower Egyptian control of Upper Egypt and held that the Delta had been subjugated by the kings of Upper Egypt, such as Scorpion (figure 1) and Narmer. This theory is reinforced by iconographical evidence such as the Narmer palette (figure 2). Anthropologists have seen the named kings merely as symbols and looked to causes such as environmental change, population pressures and economic development for the creation of the Egyptian state.

2. The Narmer palette from the Temple Area of Nekhen, Hierakonpolis. (Above) (a) One side shows the king in the white crown of Upper Egypt. (Right) (b) The other side shows the king in the red crown of Lower Egypt. (Cairo 14716.)

2

Principal sites

Most of the Predynastic cemetery sites identified along the Egyptian Nile valley have a Late Predynastic or Protodynastic component and their use often extends into the Early Dynastic period, but only the most important are mentioned in detail here, together with the principal excavated settlement sites from the south (Upper Egypt) to the north (Lower Egypt).

Elephantine still retains the name (anciently Abu) connected with the trade in ivory from Africa. The archaeological site, which has a long history dating back to the Predynastic period (Naqada II), sits astride two rocky islands at the first cataract of the Nile at Aswan, which is the furthest limit of Egypt before Nubia. The temple there was dedicated to the goddess Satet and her consort Khnum and a walled town had developed by the Old Kingdom. A German expedition has excavated extensively at the site since 1970 and Günter Dreyer revealed an early shrine set in a natural niche between the large granite boulders of the cataract, with brick walls forming rooms and a courtyard in front. This sacred area was in use until the Middle Kingdom, although it was continuously redesigned and finally filled in during the New Kingdom, when a stone temple was built above it by Tuthmosis III. Votive objects of the Protodynastic and Early Dynastic periods were found, including numerous figurines and models entirely similar to those from deposits in the temples at Hierakonpolis and Abydos.

El Kab, ancient Nekheb, where a rich Protodynastic cemetery has been excavated within the New Kingdom town enclosure by a modern Belgian expedition, is situated on the east bank of the Nile north of Edfu and opposite to **Hierakonpolis**, ancient Nekhen, on the west bank (figure 3). After British excavations from the turn of the twentieth century followed by intermittent investigations, the Americans Walter Fairservis and Michael Hoffman began work at Hierakonpolis in 1969. An overall plan of the Early Dynastic structures in the town, following the line of a building complex which leads from a large mud-brick gateway with niched façade (figure 36), was produced. Augering by Hoffman revealed Predynastic occupation at a depth of 4 metres and showed that the Nile has now receded to the east from Nekhen. Excavation of one quadrant utilising a pump revealed stratified deposits going back from the First Dynasty to Naqada I, with sherd indications of the Badarian culture. The area had obviously been sacred for a considerable time. The circular revetted structure of sandstone blocks, enclosing an artificial sand mound,

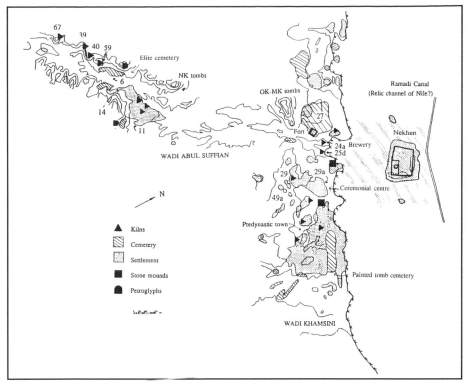

3. Site map of Hierakonpolis. (After Renée Friedman.)

4. The courtyard of the desert temple at Hierakonpolis with the mud-brick Fort in the distance. (Photograph Michael Hoffman.)

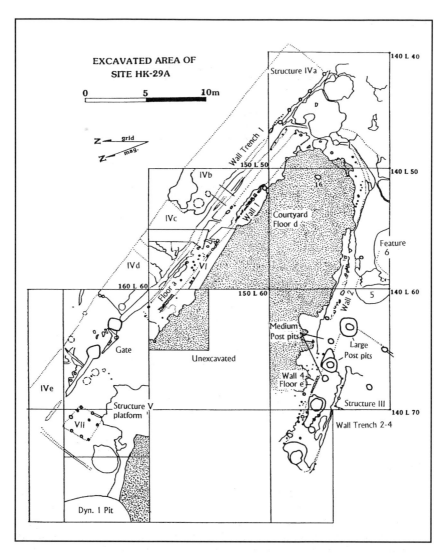

EXCAVATED AREA OF SITE HK-29A

0   5   10m

z ← grid
z ← mag.

Structure IVa

Wall Trench I

140 L 40

150 L 50

140 L 50

IVb

IVc

Wall 1

16

Courtyard Floor d

Feature 6

IVd

VI

Floor a

160 L 60

150 L 60

140 L 60

Medium Post pits

Large Post pits

Gate

Unexcavated

Wall 2

5

IVe

Wall 4 Floor e

Structure III

Structure V platform

140 L 70

VII

Wall Trench 2-4

Dyn. 1 Pit

5. Plan of the Predynastic ceremonial complex at Hierakonpolis. (After Hoffman and Friedman.)

and the limestone columns and patches of sandstone pavement found outside it by James Quibell and Frederick Green in 1898 seem to delineate an early temple. Caches of ceremonial and votive objects, notably the so-called 'Main Deposit', confirmed the site's importance in the Proto-dynastic and Early Dynastic.

Between the Wadi Abul Suffian and the Wadi Khamsin to the south there is an extensive desert-edge Predynastic town where Hoffman

6. The carved design on a bone cylinder showing large pear-shaped mace-heads on poles, Main Deposit, Hierakonpolis. (Ash. E.4714; courtesy of the Visitors of the Ashmolean Museum, Oxford.)

revealed an intriguing complex (Locality 29A) identified as a temple (figure 4), dated by ceramic analysis to Naqada IIb-IId with a Naqada III component. It consists of a large parabolic-shaped courtyard (figure 5), paved four times with smoothed clay, with a deep hole at the south end which perhaps supported a freestanding pole, possibly surmounted by the totem of a god or a ceremonial mace-head (figure 6). On the north side postholes mark a gateway, while others connect with a brick wall and various outbuildings. Opposite the gateway are four large postholes, 1.7 metres deep, which form the monumental façade of a structure 13 metres wide, possibly the original Per Wer shrine of Upper Egypt. The reconstruction of the temple (figure 7) bears a strong resemblance to the scene on the Narmer mace-head, including the serpentine brick wall (figure 8). Analysis of the faunal remains shows that adult and young cattle, sheep and goats were killed and that large

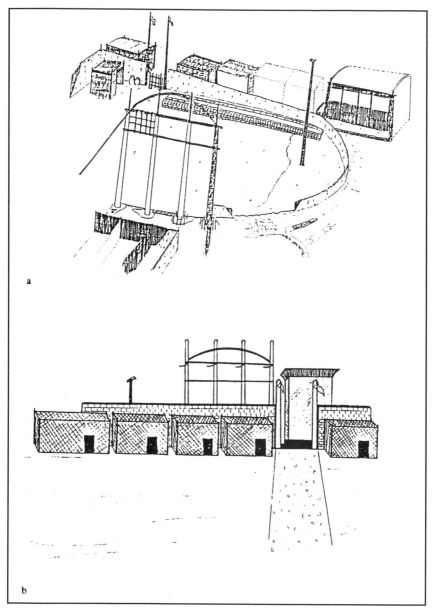

7. (a) Reconstruction of the Predynastic desert temple at Hierakonpolis. (After Hoffman.) (b) Reconstruction of the complex as approached from the Nile. (After Friedman and Genato.)

8. The mace-head of Narmer from the Main Deposit at Hierakonpolis. (Ash. E.3631; courtesy of the Visitors of the Ashmolean Museum, Oxford.)

and dangerous aquatic Nile fauna, such as perch, turtle and crocodile, were caught for use in the complex.

Hoffman also worked in a large, looted Predynastic cemetery (Locality 6) in the Wadi Abul Suffian, where, although Predynastic graves of transitional date (Naqada Ic-IIa) have been uncovered, so far classic Naqada IIcd graves have not been found. At the east end of the cemetery three large, looted Protodynastic tombs were excavated. Tomb 1 (6.5

9. Tomb 11 at Hierakonpolis looking north. (Photograph Barbara Adams.)

metres long) and Tomb 10 (4.70 metres long) are rectangular and lined with mud-brick, with postholes in the base, and were surmounted by a wood and reed building and surrounded by a picket fence. Tomb 11 (5.0 metres long, figure 9), nearer the centre of the cemetery and slightly earlier in date, retained more of its contents, including beads and amulets in exotic materials, ivory carvings, stone and pottery models of animals and humans, and reconstructable pottery. At the west end of the cemetery, near the earlier Predynastic tombs, a large rectangular tomb (Tomb 2: 6.25 metres), with a small side chamber originally sealed with two stones, was cut into the sandstone bedrock. West of Tomb 2 was the grave of three cattle with organic material around the ribs; and baboon, dog, elephant, hippopotamus and crocodile bones were also found at this end of the cemetery.

Substantial mud-brick walls of a large enclosure were excavated at **Naqada** by Petrie and Quibell in 1895-6 and this South Town is said to date to the latter part of the Gerzean (Naqada IIcd) period, as are élite tombs in a separate part (Cemetery T) of a huge cemetery behind the town. This density of occupation indicates that at some time Naqada was probably the capital of a chiefdom, until the region was absorbed by the proto-kingdom of Hierakonpolis. The smaller Ballas cemetery contained Protodynastic graves.

Petrie's aim whilst clearing the temple of Isis and Min at **Koptos** north of Thebes was to find early statues and sculptures which may have been put in pits during Ptolemaic rebuilding. In this aim he

10. Site map of Abydos with cemeteries U, B and the royal tombs of the First Dynasty. (After Petrie and Dreyer.)

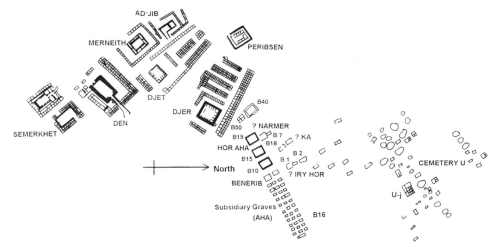

succeeded for he discovered monumental limestone statues of a bird and three lions, and parts of three statues and a head of a male fertility god. All of these appear to date from the time of Narmer.

In later periods of Egyptian history **Abydos** was thought to have been the burial place of the god Osiris because of the Archaic mud-brick tombs, particularly that of Djer, in the desert cemetery (figure 10). Therefore a monument or tomb at the site was a way of ensuring, through the favour of the god, a safe passage to the afterlife, and the potsherd-strewn early necropolis is the reason for its Arabic name, Umm el Qa'ab ('Mother of Pots'). The site has endured the work of early excavators, such as Emile Amélineau (1895-8), as well as the deprivations of looters. Apart from late Protodynastic tombs in Cemetery B, followed by the sequence of tombs of the First and Second Dynasties re-excavated by Petrie between 1899 and 1900, more recent excavation by Günter Dreyer has uncovered tombs that date from earlier in the Protodynastic (Naqada III) period and from late Naqada II. The earliest Predynastic tombs in Cemetery U, which is situated to the north of the Umm el Qa'ab, are either small unlined pits or large pits with wood linings; the later tombs are brick-lined like those of the Locality 6 cemetery at Hierakonpolis, but some of them have multiple rooms. One more elaborate tomb, U-j, consisted of twelve rooms (9.10 by 7.30

11. Tomb U-j at Abydos. (Courtesy of Günter Dreyer, German Institute of Archaeology, Cairo.)

metres), nine of which were storerooms added to the original rectangular burial chamber, containing hundreds of pottery vessels of
Egyptian and imported Canaanite ware (figure 11). The Egyptian wavy-
handled pots are inscribed with one or two large signs in black ink,
most frequently a scorpion with a plant. The burial chamber contained a
wooden shrine and an *hk3* sceptre of ivory. In one of two chambers that
had been added later alongside the tomb 150 small bone labels with
hieroglyphic signs were found (figure 44a).

The German expedition has also recleared some of the First Dynasty
tombs and in the Tomb of Den a clay seal impression was discovered
with the names of the rulers in sequence from Narmer to Aha, Djer,
Djet, Den and Queen Merneith, interspersed with the name of
Khentiamentiu, the principal god of Abydos. These names can be
paralleled by the sequence of tombs in the cemetery, which is continued
by the tombs of Adj-ib, Semerkhet and Qa'a of the First Dynasty. This
sequence has been confirmed by another seal impression found in the
tomb of Qa'a (figure 21n), and is completed by the tombs of Peribsen
and Khasekhemwy of the Second Dynasty, the latter being some way
south of the rest. As well as subsidiary graves around the tombs, it
seems that each of the royal tombs of the First and Second Dynasties in
the Umm el Qa'ab had a separate building located closer to the edge of
the floodplain and surrounded by rows of servant burials. The best-
preserved of these mud-brick funerary structures are those of the Second
Dynasty kings Peribsen and Khasekhemwy. The latter monument, the
Shunet el-Zebib, is double-walled like the Fort at Hierakonpolis and
also bears palace-façade niched panelling on the exterior of the inner
wall. Near the funerary enclosures the American Egyptologist David
O'Connor has discovered twelve pits covered with whitewashed, mud-
plastered mud-brick superstructures and containing wooden boats
between 15 and 18 metres long.

Tradition has it that the First Dynasty rulers buried at Abydos were
based at the city of This, which has not been discovered but is thought
to be near the modern town of Girga to the north. A temple of
Khentiamentiu near the alluvium at Abydos, with indications of
Predynastic occupation in the temenos (temple precinct), was excavated
by Petrie in 1901. Votive figurines, like those found at Elephantine and
Hierakonpolis, were found in pits in this temple beneath the level of
Old Kingdom mud-brick walls.

A few of the cemetery sites in the northern part of Middle Egypt east
of the Fayum basin, such as **Harageh** and **Sedment**, produced limited
quantities of pottery which is now known to be part of a Lower Egyptian
tradition which predates the spread of Upper Egyptian culture into the
north from Naqada IIc. Now that excavation has been undertaken in the

Delta and the nature of Lower Egyptian pottery types is known these types can be identified in museum collections and at Upper Egyptian sites and there is no doubt that there was also a limited cultural interchange from north to south in the Gerzean. Other sites in the north of Middle Egypt illustrate the cultural penetration of Upper Egyptian traditions into the north before the First Dynasty.

One such site, at **Abusir el-Melek**, was explored in 1902-6 by a German expedition led by Georg Möller; its findings were later published by Alexander Scharff. The large cemetery, consisting of over nine hundred excavated graves, is dated from Naqada IIcd to Naqada III. The simplest graves were oval pits and most of the people buried here were moderately affluent. There were, however, a few large, richly furnished rectangular graves, lined with mud-brick, and in these the contracted bodies were contained in coffins of pottery or wood. A few large graves were divided into rectangular chambers each containing typical grave goods, animal bones and the body of a child, and these are similar to other sites where rich graves devoted to children have been found. The pottery from this cemetery is identical to Upper Egyptian forms, notwithstanding certain differences such as the absence of black-topped red vessels and a higher percentage of black-polished ones, more typical of Lower Egyptian traditions. There is a noticeable variety of vessels made of stone, bone or ivory, and the finds include copper vessels. Flint tools, pear-shaped mace-heads, cosmetic palettes, combs and bone pins are copies of southern forms and there were some examples of small anthropomorphic and zoomorphic figurines, mainly of stone.

The large Archaic cemeteries of **Tarkhan**, which is the northernmost site of this group south of Cairo, came into use shortly before the First Dynasty. Inscriptions of Narmer and other names, presumably officials, were found by Petrie in 1911-13 in several large mastaba tombs and the spatial patterning of the valley cemetery suggests élite areas reflecting a stratified society. The numerous Early Dynastic graves here enabled Petrie to extend his relative dating system to the Third Dynasty, although by this point he used one Sequence Date for a reign.

In the Cairo area various cemeteries which date to the Early Dynastic period have been excavated on both sides of the river Nile, which has moved to the east since that time. David Jeffreys has suggested that the settlement of **Memphis** was on the west bank of the Nile close to the escarpment where the élite tombs of north Saqqara are situated and that it was abandoned in the Third Dynasty when the river receded. The location of the large First and Second Dynasty mastaba tombs on the eastern edge of the desert plateau would have made them highly visible from the cultivation. The first of these mastabas dates to the time of

12. (Top) The boat burial associated with tomb 3036 and (below) subsidiary tomb 3111 at the Early Dynastic necropolis at Saqqara. (From an archive negative in the Petrie Museum of Egyptian Archaeology, University College London; see W. B. Emery, *Great Tombs* I, Cairo, 1949.)

Aha, and then ribbon development continued north and south until the end of the First Dynasty; the mastabas of the Second Dynasty are built behind the first row. The tombs are often surrounded by single or double enclosure walls, and rows of subsidiary tombs and boat burials from the time of Aha to Den were found by Walter Emery (figure 12). Further to the north, at **Abusir**, there are smaller Early Dynastic tombs and Zaki Saad excavated three areas of Early Dynastic cemeteries on the east bank of the river opposite to the necropolis at north Saqqara.

Tell Ibrahim Awad and **el-Tell el-Iswid** in the eastern Delta have been explored since 1986 by a Dutch expedition, directed first by Edwin van den Brink and later by Willem van Haarlem. Two main chronological phases have been distinguished in the occupation levels for the Pre-dynastic and Protodynastic periods. Phase A, which is contemporary with Naqada IIcd, does not contain brick architecture, and settlement is indicated by postholes for wickerwork huts, numerous hearths and clay-lined storage pits. In phase B, contemporary with Naqada III, the remains of rectangular mud-brick buildings have survived. Judging from the pottery, the two phases seem to represent a cultural discontinuity between the indigenous Buto-Maadi cultural complex and the succeeding Upper Egyptian style, which became adopted nationally from Naqada III, although some of the pottery in phase A includes types that are known in Upper Egypt in Naqada II, such as impressed and incised wares. The *serekh* sign, which means 'to make known' in Egyptian, is derived from one niche of the recessed and buttressed brick wall of the palace façade, which was itself a copy of earlier reed structures that became associated with royalty. Fragments of pottery with serekhs, including the double falcon type without a name and others enclosing the signs for Ka and Narmer, were found at Tell Ibrahim Awad. Another settlement site in the eastern Delta which has produced some evidence for the cultural superimposition of Upper Egyptian pottery types over Lower Egyptian wares is **Mendes**, where work was resumed by Robert Wenke between 1990 and 1992.

Minshat Abu Omar is a late Predynastic to Early Dynastic necro-polis of Naqada culture type in the eastern part of the Delta excavated between 1978 and 1990 by a German expedition directed by Dietrich Wildung and Karla Kroeper. The burial ground dates back to Naqada IId and the artefacts are purely Upper Egyptian in style. The excavators identified four groups among the 420 burials, varying from one another in the size of the graves, the wealth of the furnishings, the pottery and above all the orientation of the bodies laid in them; these may be arbitrary divisions as the assemblages of artefacts cannot be so divided elsewhere. The construction of the graves also varied, from ordinary pits to those with their walls lined with matting and mud and roofed with mats. The fourth and youngest group included some rectangular graves, 6 by 4.5 metres, lined with mud-brick and divided into two chambers roofed with wooden beams and layers of mats (figure 13). The bodies, particularly those in the larger graves, were laid in rectangular coffins made of wood, reed or plaster/mud. In general, later graves were not only larger but also contained more and richer offerings; some of those graves were clearly distinguishable as belonging to the

13. Tomb 1450 at Minshat Abu Omar excavated to show the subterranean structure of the mud-brick walls lining the grave. (Courtesy of Dietrich Wildung, German East Delta Expedition.)

élite. Besides various types of Upper Egyptian pottery, including those with serekhs, and Palestinian forms, there were particularly remarkable models of boats and a bone casket with decoration resembling a palace façade, numerous palettes, a variety of stone vessels, amulets and personal finery.

Another potentially informative large Protodynastic and Early Dynastic cemetery is being excavated by Fekri Hassan at **Kafr Hassan Dawood** on the southern edge of the Wadi Tumilat. It has yielded nearly a thousand burials, signs of socio-economic differentiation and pottery with the name of Narmer.

Buto (Tell el Fara'in), a sacred city in pharaonic times, in the north-western part of the Delta, has been explored since 1983 by a German expedition directed originally by Thomas von der Way and later by Dina Faltings. The oldest two layers of the stratified settlement, which are reached with the aid of pumps, are contemporary with Naqada IIb and IIc-d respectively, and both clearly belong to the Lower Egyptian Buto-Maadi cultural complex. The next layer is transitional, containing a mix of northern and southern material. From Naqada IId2 the amount of Lower Egyptian pottery gradually decreases in favour of Upper Egyptian types, as do the flint tools. Similar changes can also be observed in building methods, although there is no hiatus in settlement here nor any distinct layer of destruction which might testify to an invasion and conquest and to the extermination of the population of Lower Egypt. On the contrary, the occurrence side by side of elements characteristic of the two cultural complexes suggests a peaceful coexistence and gradual infiltration of the Upper Egyptian population into the Delta territory long before the traditionally accepted date of the unification of Egypt. The youngest strata, which are exclusively within the Naqada cultural tradition, date to the period between Naqada IId2 and the decline of the First Dynasty. A sequence of large rectangular residential and domestic mud-brick buildings was excavated and some finds, such as architectural elements and pottery, seem to point to commercial relations with northern Syria and Mesopotamia.

3

Material culture and writing

Although there is no doubt that the material culture of the Protodynastic period exhibits both a continuation of Predynastic types and precursors to Dynastic styles, a growing difference in quality, size and quantity of certain types of object can be observed. This trend is evident in the development of some larger graves with richer grave goods in some cemeteries from the Gerzean (Naqada II) period onwards. By the time that royalty was established the grand tombs and separate funerary enclosures were surrounded by the smaller tombs of sacrificed servants. Socio-economic differentiation is not always easy to analyse because of the negative evidence of plundered cemeteries and because most statistical studies have concentrated on the region north of Armant, but there do seem to be increased numbers of élite graves and clusters of graves in important places, such as Hierakonpolis, Naqada, Abydos and Minshat Abu Omar, from the Gerzean period. This is taken to indicate the growth of a ruling class within society, with first local chieftains, then regional leaders and finally a king. The expression of this ruling class is epitomised by the few commemorative scenes that have remained; their significance is discussed in the next chapter.

Pottery remains the key artefact type for relative dating and, apart from changes in shape, it also exhibits technological improvements which resulted from experiments undertaken at the end of the Naqada II phase of the Predynastic. The wares identified for the Predynastic divide into those made of Nile silt pottery, from which, by the addition of temper, and using different firing methods and surface finish, the potters produced the well-known types of Upper Egypt such as the straw-tempered ('Rough' class), black-topped red (B class), polished red (P class) and painted (C class) vessels. Detailed study of pottery from the settlements of Upper Egypt by Renée Friedman has made clear that there were local traditions in utilitarian wares until Naqada IIc, when the methodology of adding chaff temper developed at Hierakonpolis took over at other sites. Excavations in Lower Egyptian sites such as Maadi and Buto have enabled the identification of Nile silt wares made in the north during the Predynastic, which are chiefly distinguished by the use of fibre temper and a black or brown surface finish.

During the 1980s geochemical ceramic analysis undertaken by Ralph Allen and Hany Hamroush at Hierakonpolis also identified a technologically advanced ware: Nile silt tempered with crushed calcium carbonate. This additive included calcium salts which aided the vitrification process to produce a hard pottery that fires pink-orange. The Gerzean settlement evidence indicates that this was the first marl ware produced at Hierakonpolis and it is the distinctive ware of the Proto-dynastic period there and at other sites in Upper Egypt. Thus the ceramic repertoire of the Protodynastic period may include straw-tempered Nile silt, sandy marl, mixed marl and Nile silt clay, and crushed calcium carbonate tempered Nile silt vessels. The last 'hard orange' fabric is made into large and medium storage and cylinder jars, some of which are painted in red, bowls and jars with a red surface coating which copy the earlier polished red and black-topped red pottery (figure 14) and bowls with an orange-red coating decorated with a streak burnish. All

14. A black-topped orange *hes* pottery jar and a model of the same type, Main Deposit, Hierakonpolis. (Courtesy of the Petrie Museum of Egyptian Archaeology, University College, London. UC.15074 and UC.15094.)

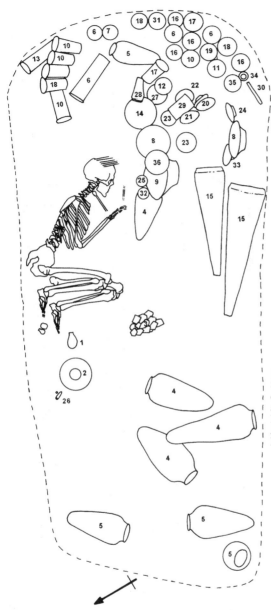

15. (a) (Left) Plan of El Kab grave 85. (b) (Opposite page) Contents of grave 85: pottery, stone vases and palettes. (After Stan Hendrickx, *El Kab V: The Naqada III Cemetery*, 1994, plates LXIV, LXV.)

of these wares were grouped together by Petrie into his L class, which serves to identify a chronological phase rather than a typological entity by clay fabric and temper.

The pivotal types in Petrie's Sequence Dating scheme were the wavy-

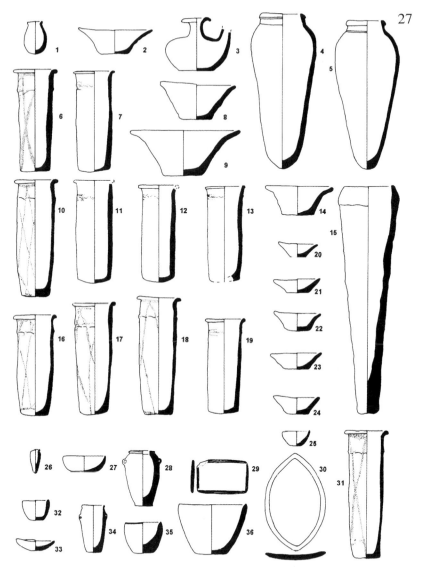

handled jars, which he put into a separate W class although they include the same fabrics as L class, and they are still relied upon in present relative dating methodology. Thus the large Protodynastic grave 85 (figure 15) excavated at El Kab, which is put in his Naqada IIIA2 by Stan Hendrickx, has cylinder jars with the evolved type of wavy handle extending around the circumference of the jar; some of them have the red, so-called net painting. The grave also contained typical straw-tempered bowls and storage vessels and crushed calcium carbonate tempered storage jars. It is the richest grave in the El Kab cemetery, which is richer overall than other cemeteries known in Upper Egypt, and its pottery compares with the assemblage from the élite tomb 11 at Hierakonpolis.

Modern methods of ceramic study, which involve a careful identification of the fabric by clay and temper type, often corroborated by petrographic and neutron activation analysis and X-ray diffraction, enable archaeologists to single out pottery 'foreign' to the sites they are excavating. This is most useful in the identification of imported pottery from places such as Canaan, or in differentiating between Lower and Upper Egyptian pottery at opposite ends of the country. It has become obvious that fashion was the mother of invention during this period of cultural expansion and that imported pottery was copied in local fabrics to meet demand or to satisfy curiosity for the unusual.

Analyses of stone tools from the stratified sequences of settlement sites are augmenting the limited repertoire of flints found in cemeteries. Like the pottery, the regional 'Buto-Maadi culture' lithic repertoire of the Delta was superseded by Upper Egyptian types in Naqada IIcd and rare types such as fine bifacial and ripple-flaked tools were imported. It seems that primary production took place at manufacturing centres, from which finished or semi-finished artefacts were distributed. The industrial scale quantity of *debitage* (chips left over from the flaking process) indicates that the late Gerzean desert temple at Hierakonpolis was such a production centre, where specialised craftsmen made not only bifacial and rippled knives but also micro-drills for bead making. The production of flint artefacts in the Protodynastic decreased to about one-tenth of what it had been during the Gerzean, no doubt because of the expansion of metal tool production. The secondary types were non-twisted blade and bifacial pieces, which were made into sickle blades and knives, and flakes, which were also made into tools. Specialised tools, such as crescent tools for the manufacture of stone vases, micro-drills and large scrapers, also persisted. In the First Dynasty the knives which developed exaggerated 'cut-out' handles have been identified as ritual slaughtering tools for temple sacrifice (figure 16), and the truncated blades with retouched ends, predominantly found in grave or offering contexts, may have served a cosmetic purpose. Intricate pressure-flaked arrowheads of flint and crystal have also been found in early royal tombs.

Other aspects of material culture are inextricably linked. The working of stone for vases and statuary would not have been possible without the development of metallurgy for the production of drills, chisels, adzes and saws (figure 17). Copper working led to the exploitation of

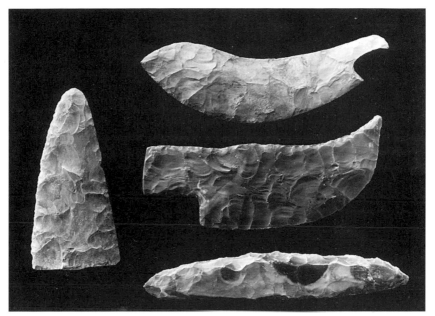

16. Flint knives from tombs 619, 1982, 1266 and 1247 at Tarkhan, First Dynasty. (From an archive negative in the Petrie Museum of Egyptian Archaeology, University College London; see W. M. F. Petrie, *Tarkhan* II, 1914, plate VI, 9.)

17. Copper axe with the name of Ka-hotep, copper adzc with the serekh of Djet, whetstone, copper chisel and larger axe, from the 'Tombs of the Courtiers', Abydos, First Dynasty. (Courtesy of the Petrie Museum of Egyptian Archaeology, University College London. UC.16173-16177.)

mineral resources in the eastern desert and the Sinai. The copper ore, malachite, provided the green colouring used in the production of early faience, which is a fired quartz-based paste used to make figurines and vases. All of these technological methods were developed in the Predynastic, refined in the Protodynastic, and a commonplace part of the economy in the early unified state.

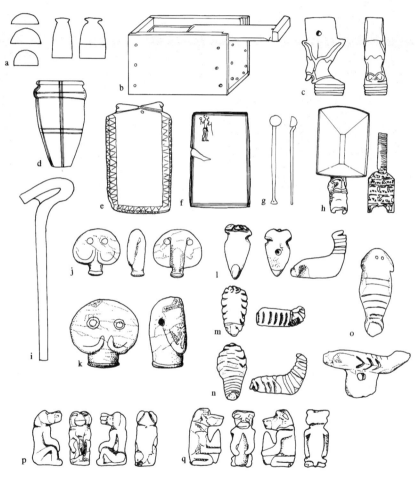

18. (a) Ivory gaming pieces. (b) Wooden box with sliding lid. (c) Ivory bull's leg from a box or bed. (d) Ivory vase. (e, f) 'Slate' palettes. (g, h) Ivory spoons, Tarkhan (after Petrie). (i) Ivory sceptre, tomb U-j, Abydos (after Dreyer). (j) Limestone bull's head, city of Nekhen (after Hoffman). (k) Serpentine bull's head. (l, m, n, o) Limestone, faience and pottery scorpions. (p, q) Faience baboons, Main Deposit, Hierakonpolis (after Adams).

19. Votive figures of a man in haematite, faience figures of a wild boar and a pelican and two ornate limestone vases from the Main Deposit, Hierakonpolis. (From an archive negative in the Petrie Museum of Egyptian Archaeology, University College London.)

Another aspect of social stratification is that stone vessels, greywacke (slate) cosmetic palettes, fine flint knives, beads and amulets are not very frequent in middle-class burials, however many pots may be contained in a grave. The ordinary stone vases are usually made of relatively soft stone such as calcite, or limestone, and serpentine. The harder and more difficult stones such as basalt, which was fashionable in Naqada I-II, and breccia are rarely used. The greywacke palettes from ordinary graves are sometimes degenerate zoomorphic shapes such as fish, but frequently only misshapen ovals, and by the First Dynasty they became utilitarian rectangles. A reduced quantity of objects carved in bone and ivory, such as hairpins, spoons and vessels, has been observed in cemeteries. In the larger élite graves, however, fine stone vases and delicate ivory carving in the form of decorated boxes, gaming pieces and a sceptre have been found (figure 18). Tomb 11 at Hierakonpolis also contained ivory carvings, a fine basalt cup and figurines in pottery and stone, as well as a range of jewellery in carnelian, garnet, faience, gold, silver, turquoise and lapis lazuli. In addition to the large decorated palettes and mace-heads, larger, sometimes decorated stone vases in hard stone such as porphyry and enormous flint knives up to 64 cm long have been found in temples, as at Hierakonpolis. There and at Abydos votive figurines were made in elephant and hippopotamus ivory and bone, whilst pottery, stone and faience models were found at those temples and at Elephantine (figure 19). Faience was also used to make wall tiles and large beads, the components of hangings, providing tantalising glimpses of the blue-green decor of early sacred buildings. Although rare in graves, quantities of both disc- and pear-shaped stone mace-heads of normal size were deposited in the temple at Hierakonpolis. Fragments of pear-shaped mace-heads were also found in the lower levels of the temples at Abydos and Koptos.

Wood is a relatively scarce natural resource in Egypt but it was used extensively in the construction of the increasingly large Protodynastic

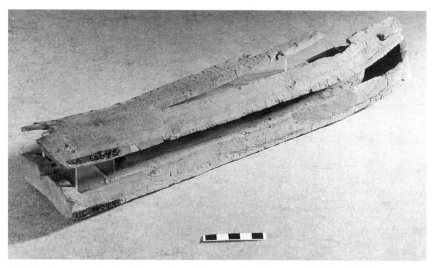

20. Wooden case in the shape of an *s3* (protection) sign, tomb 213, Tarkhan, time of Merneith, First Dynasty. (UC.16075.)

graves, which were lined with mud-brick and then roofed with planks, often supported by posts in the centre of the tombs. The tombs were then enclosed by wooden posts and wattle fences. Large posts and other timber elements were also used in domestic and religious architecture, as well as for boat planking, and it has been suggested that cedar was imported from Lebanon before the First Dynasty. Poor-quality native timber was produced from acacia and tamarisk and used to make furniture such as beds with bull's legs, stools and boxes (figure 20). Fragments which Petrie gleaned from the plundered First Dynasty royal tombs at Abydos indicate that wood-carving was intricate and highly developed, with ornate decoration often copying basketry, and that ebony, a harder wood, was imported in small quantities from Ethiopia.

The remains of textiles from Predynastic and Protodynastic graves are rare, perhaps because of the accidents of preservation, or because they were a valuable commodity stolen from graves very early, but it is obvious from later tomb scenes and grave goods that woven linen was economically important even as bales of cloth. Moreover it seems that the bone labels found in tomb U-j at Abydos which have incised numerals

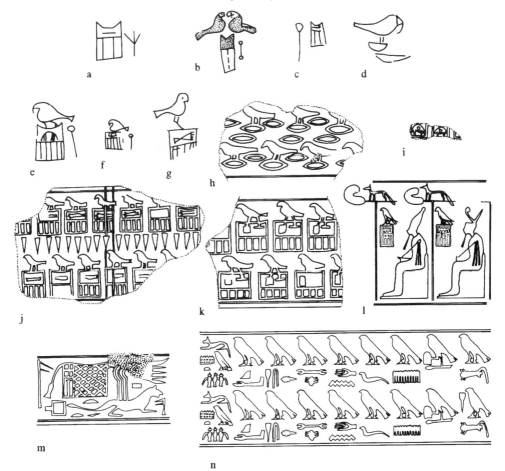

21. Royal names on pottery (a-g) and seals (h-n): (a-c) early serekhs; (d, h) Iry Hor (Ro); (e, i) Ka; (f) Crocodile; (g, j) Narmer; (k) Hor Aha; (l) Djer; (m) Per Wer shrine of Upper Egypt with lion; (n) king-list of the First Dynasty to Qa'a. (After Petrie, Kaiser and Dreyer.)

as well as hieroglyphic signs were meant to indicate sizes of webs of cloth that formed part of the original grave goods (figure 44a). Some later bone or ivory labels have sandals incised on the back (figure 44d), indicating that they were originally associated with leather footwear no longer extant. Wooden sandal trays were found in the First Dynasty cemetery at Tarkhan.

The introduction of writing

Owing to the lack of earlier evidence, the appearance of Egyptian writing was until recently believed to have been the consequence of the emergence of a united, centrally governed state – a secondary phenomenon which developed under the stimulus of Asiatic contact. Now the first signs of writing in tomb U-j at Abydos, dated to Naqada IIIa2, contradict this theory and point to the existence of a fairly advanced administration before 3200 BC. Thus the introduction of writing is one more proof of the fact that the formation of a state is the last stage and not the first link from which everything begins. Not only were the alphabetic signs used by the early rulers an important way of legitimising their power but also they played an essential role in the bureaucracy which controlled the economy.

The impressions of cylinder seals, incised with early hieroglyphs, appear on clay sealings on pottery vessels to denote their ownership or to define their contents or purpose. Oil was an extremely important commodity and some of

22. Large pottery jar with an incised serekh of Narmer, tomb 414, Tarkhan. (Courtesy of the Petrie Museum of Egyptian Archaeology, University College London. UC.16083.)

the extant First Dynasty bone and ebony inscribed labels which record religious events were primarily identification tags for jars of oil. The names of early monarchs, incised into pottery vessels or as seal impressions (figure 21), may prove the existence of central control over the distribution of goods in particularly great demand, which were imported and exported by the state. In a similar way, the so-called potmarks seem to testify to the existence of a bureaucracy dealing with the importation and distribution of certain goods. This is indicated by the fact that these marks were incised into imported pottery after it had been fired and probably not before its arrival in Egypt (figure 34).

Hieroglyphic signs and the introduction of Egyptian writing were therefore connected with the appearance of the first central institutions of the emerging state, chiefly resulting from the development of economy and trade.

4

Interpretation of decorative devices

Mankind has produced art since the dawn of prehistory, but even the petroglyphs and rock paintings created by palaeolithic hunters cannot be relied upon as historical representations which reflect actual happenings. They could be free interpretations of a subject, embellished versions of desired occurrences. The question is whether they should be discussed in terms of history, culture or religion, and the same problem is incurred when dealing with early Egyptian art. Here there are no firm grounds for establishing a method of interpreting the paintings and reliefs produced towards the end of the Predynastic period. They may be historical sources or they may be generalising and mythologising the processes occurring along the Nile valley. An additional difficulty arises from the fact that the later art of pharaonic Egypt seems to draw numerous influences from the period of state formation. Thus investigators of the origins of Egyptian art can consider several questions only hypothetically. It should be kept in mind that there is a paucity of sources and a long span of time (at least five hundred years) between the oldest and the youngest of these extant objects. The only objective method is a literal analysis of the subject matter of a representation without yielding to the temptation of seeking hidden or disguised meanings in it, and using great caution when referring to the images known from a later time.

The main feature that all the most important representations dating from the late Predynastic and Early Dynastic periods have in common is their direct or indirect connection with an individual who can justifiably be called a ruler, at first the person who was the head of a local community, and later the head of a state. The painted linen from Gebelein (figure 23) and the decorated grave at Hierakonpolis seem to be the oldest two-dimensional scenes that are dated fairly firmly. The former, attributed to the Naqada Ic-IIa period, is preserved only as fragments, but the beginnings of the thematic division of scenes making up a composition can be discerned: a possible dance, a hunt and a procession of boats. The essential fragment shows the last of these. In one boat there is a seated figure, wrapped in a mantle resembling the later Heb-Sed ritual attire, with a flail in one hand. In the boat depicted below, a kneeling man can be seen with his hands tied behind his back, while a mace is suspended over his head.

The largest and most complex Predynastic scene appears in a unique painting from tomb 100 at Hierakonpolis (figure 24a), which was excavated by Green in a desert-edge Gerzean cemetery near the Wadi

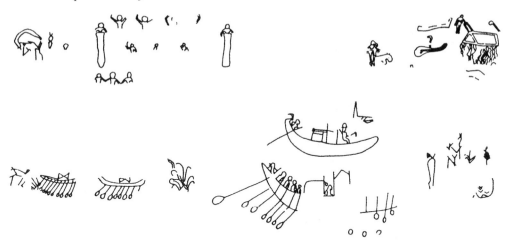

23. The painted design on linen from a tomb at Gebelein. (After B. Williams and T. J. Logan, *Journal of Near Eastern Studies* 46, 1987, figure 15. Turin Museum N. Suppl. 17.138.)

Khamsin on the south edge of the Hierakonpolis concession and is dated to Naqada IIc. It shows three principal subjects probably connected with the person buried in the grave – a hunt, a combat and a triumph – as well as a procession of boats, including elements of the ruler's ritual. The last cycle may be analysed in two groups. The hunting scenes are chiefly found in the upper corners of the depiction; the one on the right side, which shows a hunt with beaters and a bull being lassoed, is particularly developed (figure 24b). The bottom left-hand part of the painting depicts a combat and triumph (figure 24c). For the first time in Egyptian art the motif of a ruler smiting tied and kneeling captives with a mace appears, a subject which is present in royal iconography throughout Egyptian civilisation and into the Roman period. Close to this motif another, more controversial one is encountered – a hero strangling confronted lions. For a long time this figure was regarded as a proof of Mesopotamian influences in Predynastic Egypt, but here he may be seen as the 'Lord of Animals'.

The cycle occupying the middle part of the painting, conventionally called a procession of boats, can be analysed as two sequences. The first is formed by the upper vessels and figures in their immediate entourage. On the back cabin of the largest of the vessels at the top there is a superstructure of light materials (figure 24d), known from numerous depictions of a slightly later date on mace-heads and labels. Particularly important are those belonging to king Den of the First Dynasty, which depict the ruler at first seated in such a kiosk and next performing the

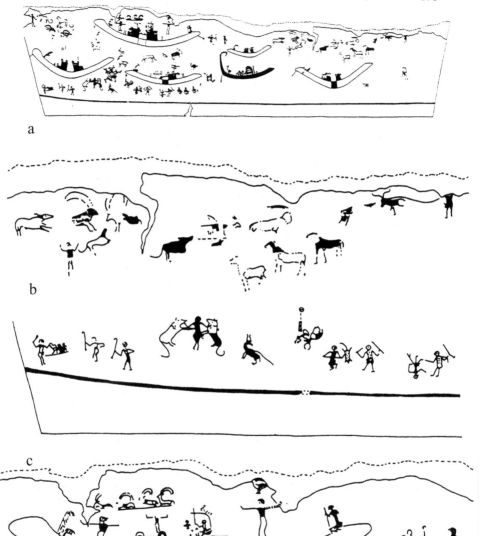

a

b

c

d

24. (Above and opposite page) (a) The painted decoration of tomb 100 at Hierakonpolis. (b-g) Details of the scene. (After J. E. Quibell and F. W. Green, *Hierakonpolis* II, 1902, plates LXXV-LXXIX.)

e

ritual Heb-Sed race of renewal (figure 44e). The connection with the ruler's festival is emphasised in the tomb painting by the presence inside the kiosk of the figure of a running man and the outline of a structure which may have been a throne. Represented in front of the kiosk is a seated figure, perhaps the prototype of the later *repit* (image). Three female figures above the boat may be performing a kind of dance. Behind the boat are fragments of two human figures. The one on the left with a flail and stick in his hands may have been running. Opposite to

f   g

him is a long-haired or wigged man, resembling the 'scribe' on the Narmer palette (figure 2).

The second sequence is formed by the remaining four boats, of which the two in the middle are the most remarkable (figure 24e). The vessel on the left is the only one equipped with the so-called standard, similar to those present on decorated (D class) pottery. On its prow in a small cabin (figure 24f) there are three red-painted forms lying one above another; these may be human figures, an identification reinforced by the use of red in this painting for representing men. The women seated below the boat on the left may have been mourners or musicians. These could be the same three figures in the scene above who took part in the Heb-Sed rituals, but in a changed mode now related to a funeral. Although the next boat differs from the others both in shape and colour, the difference derives from dissimilar materials and construction techniques, as the idea of a Mesopotamian provenance for vessels of this type is no longer tenable. This black boat is also noteworthy for a cabin on its prow, with a seated figure in white attire, probably a ruler (figure 24g). The back cabin departs from the usual shape, resembling the structure visible in the right-hand corner of the label from Naqada (figure 44c), believed to be connected with a funeral. In its horizontally divided interior there is a grey object which may represent a corpse wrapped in a shroud. The whole of this section of the scene might therefore be associated with the rituals performed after the ruler's death.

This much attention has been given to parts of the Hierakonpolis painting in order to show that in all later monuments dating from the Protodynastic and Early Dynastic periods a kind of replication of the subjects appearing here for the first time is encountered. The zoomorphic scenes occur on some palettes and knife-handles. The decoration of the

25. The Two Dog palette, Main Deposit, Hierakonpolis. (Ash. E.3924; from an archive negative in the Petrie Museum of Egyptian Archaeology, University College London.)

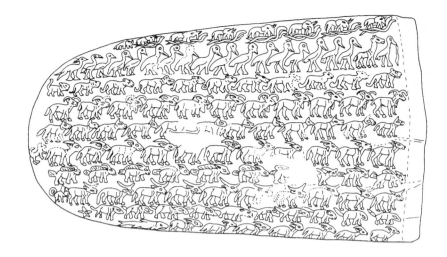

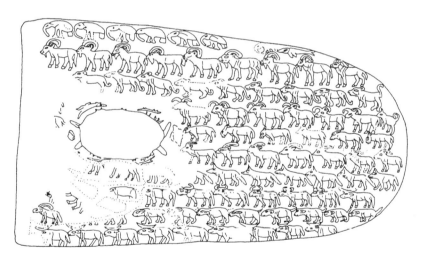

26. The Brooklyn knife-handle. (After W. Needler, *Predynastic and Archaic Egypt in the Brooklyn Museum,* 1984, page 154. Brooklyn 09.989.118.)

first group of objects reveals fairly developed hunting scenes: for instance, the Two Dog palette from Hierakonpolis (figure 25) and the Hunter's palette (BM.EA20790 and 20792, and Louvre E11254) are both composed in a characteristic manner as if the artist observed them from high above. This recalls a fragment on the right side of the Hierakonpolis tomb painting. Characteristically, real and fantastic animals appear in these scenes side by side, perhaps symbolising natural forces. On the other hand, the knife-handles in the Brooklyn (figure 26)

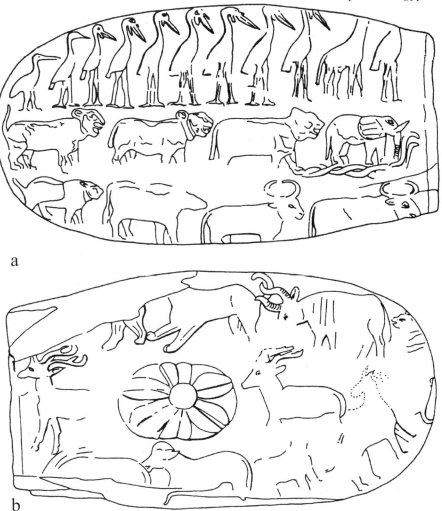

a

b

27. The Carnarvon knife-handle: (a) flat side; (b) side with boss. (After G. Bénédite, *Journal of Egyptian Archaeology,* volume 5, 1918, plates 1-2. Metropolitan Museum of Art 26.7.1281.)

and Pitt-Rivers museums are ornamented with linear sequences of animals, resembling those on decorated pottery, or the animal frieze above the largest boat in tomb 100. There is a kind of contraction of these scenes, composed of what seem to be the most significant motifs, in the Carnarvon handle (figure 27) and the Louvre palette (Louvre

E11052). The hero strangling the lions in the Hierakonpolis painting has usually been compared to a similar scene on the Gebel el-Arak knife-handle (figure 38), but there he is clearly wearing Sumerian attire, whereas in the painting he has only the penis-sheath characteristic of Predynastic Egyptian representations. The zoomorphic scene below the hero on the knife-handle is composed in a shorter and more symbolic manner than those mentioned before. Nonetheless, the whole of this side of the handle's decoration may suggest the desire to render domination over the world of animals.

Of the remaining subjects present in Protodynastic and Early Dynastic art, the most popular is a triumph over the human enemies of the ruler, which appears in a more or less disguised form in all monuments from this period. Most frequently the victorious figure is shown raising his mace to strike the kneeling or escorted captive. Examples of this kind are encountered on the Gebel el-Arak knife-handle (figure 38), on the Narmer palette (figure 2) and on cylinders from Hierakonpolis (figures 28 and 29). The ruler in the form of an animal triumphs over a naked enemy on the Battlefield (figure 40), Bull and Narmer palettes. Sometimes a triumph is represented in a more symbolic manner: the

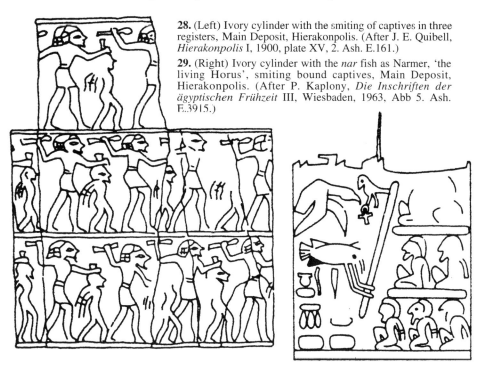

28. (Left) Ivory cylinder with the smiting of captives in three registers, Main Deposit, Hierakonpolis. (After J. E. Quibell, *Hierakonpolis* I, 1900, plate XV, 2. Ash. E.161.)

29. (Right) Ivory cylinder with the *nar* fish as Narmer, 'the living Horus', smiting bound captives, Main Deposit, Hierakonpolis. (After P. Kaplony, *Die Inschriften der ägyptischen Frühzeit* III, Wiesbaden, 1963, Abb 5. Ash. F.3915.)

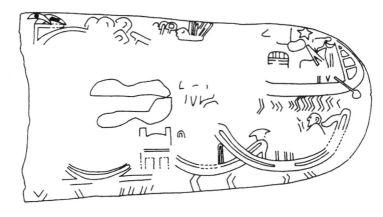

a

b

30. The Metropolitan knife-handle: (a) boss side; (b) flat side. (After B. Williams and T. J. Logan, *Journal of Near Eastern Studies* 46, 1987, figures 1-2. MMA.26.2.411.)

standards of the nomes hold the rope binding the captive on the Bull palette, or the *rekhyt* birds, symbolising the vanquished, are hung by the neck from the standards, as on the Scorpion mace-head (figure 1). In these examples the depiction clearly refers to the triumph of the ruler and his helpers over an indefinite enemy. Even the specific hieroglyphic signs describing enemies on Narmer's monuments cannot be associated with any actual historical events and must have served as a warning or indication of the claim to domination over neighbours. The entire repertoire, probably never intended for viewing by the general public, should be considered in terms of symbolism and propaganda.

Similarly the rituals connected with a living or dead ruler are continued in art, though with a varying intensity and in an increasingly symbolic form. The presence of domed structures and 'standards' in the boats with tall prows and sterns on the Gebel el-Arak handle may be somehow related to a funeral, whereas the boats with the upcurved prow and stern are provided with cabins recalling the Heb-Sed kiosk. All the scenes on the knife-handle may be a kind of contraction of the subjects known from tomb 100 at Hierakonpolis. However, the subjects present on the Metropolitan handle (figure 30) have been reduced, as far as can be judged from their poor state of preservation, to the triumph and both varieties of the procession of boats. In most monuments of a later date the reduction of subjects progresses, triumphal scenes and symbols predominating. The Scorpion mace-head is a sole exception; here a triumph has been limited to the uppermost register of the depiction, whereas the remaining scenes seem to be linked with the celebration of the jubilee festival of the king. The Abu Gurob temple reliefs, showing king Niuscrre of the Fifth Dynasty during his Hed-Sed celebrations, also represent him undertaking some building activity just like the king on the Scorpion mace-head. The First Dynasty labels seem to continue the depiction of the subjects discussed above; that from the tomb of queen Neith-hotep may concern the ceremonies connected with a funeral, while others also bearing the name of Aha may refer to triumph and cult scenes (figure 44b-c). Similar themes can be found on labels from the time of Djer and Den, but they are characterised by the reduction of depictions to one subject. The reduction of representations to only a few subjects can be observed even in the earliest scenes, and their considerable simplification is manifested in the copying of only a few motifs. This decrease in the number of subjects progresses during the Protodynastic and in the early historical period it reaches the point of reduction to scenes directly related with the ruler. At the same time the scenes become an expression of the embodiment of the ruler's qualities and perhaps were used in the rituals relating to him as he accumulated in himself all power and somehow imparted it to his subjects. He held sway over the animal world and through the renewal of his own strength during the Heb-Sed ritual ensured the same to other members of society. It is also remarkable that the same motifs lasted for so long, surviving for hundreds or even thousands of years from their creation. There remains the question of whether they were understood identically in the course of the entire history of Egyptian civilisation, or whether in later times the scenes with the triumphant pharaoh were seen as an ornament in which the primary content remained hidden and was not always brought into prominence. Instead, one merely discerns the outer signs of the power of the king and state. Equally characteristic is the relatively late appearance of a deity in a clear-cut form. Apart from the standards, which may be fetishes rather than images of gods, they are practically indiscernible until the time of Narmer. A god can appear as the king's attendant, for example Horus the falcon on the Narmer palette. The ruler is sometimes represented in the form of an animal force such as a bull or a catfish (figure 29). Such representations aim not so much at demonstrating the divinity of the king as at giving the impression of strength, wildness and unbridledness, the properties characteristic of these animals. Nor are the depictions of the chapels of that time clearly defined. They may have been connected with a god or fetish (figure 21m), but they could equally well have served the cult or the rituals related to the ruler as on the Aha label from Abydos (figure 44b).

Three-dimensional representations

Unlike bas-relief or painting, sculpture in the round is represented by much fewer large-scale monuments during this transitional period. Only a few statues of gods and kings have been preserved or were created at all, so this category of art is mostly concerned with figurines and models.

The most important monuments of three-dimensional sculpture are the

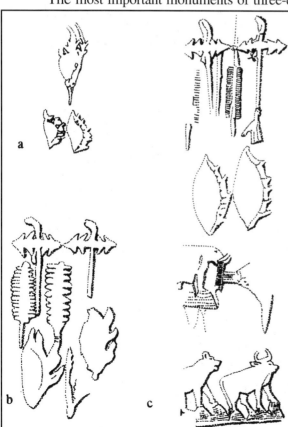

colossi from Koptos. Fragments of three limestone statues (Ashmolean 1894.-105d, 105e; Cairo JdE3-0770 bis 1), each over 4 metres tall and weighing 2 tons, in the form of flattened cylinders, were discovered by Petrie in the temple of Isis and Min in 1894. Each represented a male figure holding a stick or flail (now lost) in one hand and the base of his erect penis in the other; a separate penis, which was inserted into the round socket

31. Reliefs on the colossal statues of Min found at Koptos: (a) bovid head and Red Sea mussel shells on Ashmolean 1894.105d; (b) Min emblems, saws from sawfish and shells on Ashmolean 1894.104e (see front cover); (c) Min emblems, an ostrich, shells, an elephant, a possible bird and a hyena and bull on conical hills on Cairo 30770 bis 1. (After W. M. F. Petrie, *Koptos*, 1896, plate III.)

32. Monumental limestone lion figures reconstructed by Richard Jaeschke from fragments found in the temple at Koptos, probably dating to the time of Narmer, Naqada IIIc. (Courtesy of the Petrie Museum of Egyptian Archaeology, University College London. UC.35294A and B.)

on the statue, is now in the Ashmolean Museum in Oxford (Ash.1894.105f). There is also a head in Oxford (Ash.1894.105c), which indicates that the divinity wore a false beard, although the face is battered away. The naked torsos were girded with wide belts and their right sides are engraved with symbols: stag heads, Pteroceras shells, a standard with the sign of Min, an elephant, a hyena, and a bull on hills (figure 31). In view of the possible presence of Narmer's name on one of them, these objects may have been executed in his time at the latest. Their exceptional character has prompted speculation concerning the temple, chapel or cult circle in which they could have stood. The original existence of a shrine of Upper Egypt at Koptos, which is known from depictions on early sealings to have been fronted by lions (figure 21m), is emphasised by the three monumental lion statues which were also found there by Petrie. The two largest, which are nearly 1.5 metres long, are in University College London (figure 32); the open mouth with bared teeth, the ruff and the tail curled over the back indicate that they date stylistically from the end of the Protodynastic period to the beginning of the First Dynasty, contemporary with Narmer.

There is only one figure of a ruler from an excavated context known for this period; it is a small ivory statuette from Abydos representing a seated king in the crown of Upper Egypt, wrapped in the robes of the Heb-Sed festival (BM.EA37996). Human figurines made of stone, faience, bone, ivory and terracotta have been excavated in the main sites of Upper Egypt, in both funerary and settlement contexts. They frequently show bearded and bald men, tied and kneeling captives, children with a finger in the mouth, and naked or dressed women. These, together with models of boats, litters, plants and vessels, are elements familiar from two-dimensional art. There are also numerous sculptures of animals and birds, both wild and domestic; and figures of lions, baboons and scorpions with raised tails appear to have been particularly important (figure 18 l-q).

The appraisal of these objects is far from easy or unequivocal. The majority of the figures come from temple areas at Elephantine, Hierakonpolis and Abydos not connected with the cult of the dead and should be considered as votive offerings. This is obvious in the case of the model plants, such as lotus flowers and seeds, the models of vessels with contents and the portable kiosks or shrines. Some were no doubt connected directly with a deity, such as the falcon figures at Hierakonpolis for Horus of Nekhen, and the baboons which seemed to have honoured a divinity called Hedjwer, the 'Great White'; others, such as the scorpions, are less clearly so.

5

Foreign contacts

While reciprocal contact between Egypt and Palestine has always been accepted, the question of connections with, and possible influences from, the territories lying further to the east has been a matter of contention. There were two principal opinions, one which saw the origins of Nilotic civilisation based on an autonomous development, and the other discerning inspiration for the fundamental elements of Egyptian civilisation as impulses coming from south-western Asia, and especially from the territories with the most developed culture, Mesopotamia and Elam.

With regard to Egyptian relationships with Canaan during the late Predynastic, Protodynastic and Early Dynastic periods, there is now a wealth of material from excavations in Israel, the Sinai and Egypt (figure 33). These continually growing data are being augmented by the re-study and analysis of material in museum collections from earlier excavations. Excavators were sometimes aware that they had discovered imported Canaanite pottery, particularly when it was of a distinctive type with applied surface decoration such as a wavy handle, knob or burnish pattern (figure 34). The question of identification as either a true import or an Egyptian copy tended to be argued on purely stylistic grounds but this hit-and-miss art-historical approach has given way to scientific analysis which can identify the source of the clay and temper.

On the Canaanite side an interesting phenomenon was discovered through the petrographic analyses of Naomi Porat, who worked on the pottery from various sites in southern Canaan in the late 1980s. She found that, in addition to the imported Egyptian wares made of Nile silt, Egyptian shapes were copied in native clays at certain sites such as Tell Erani, En Besor, Lachish and Farah in southern Palestine (figure 33f-n). Her results have been augmented by the discoveries of hybrid wares from sites along the northern Sinai trade route by Eliezer Oren. Egyptian pottery and other artefacts, such as stone vases, palettes and clay sealings with impressions, as well as the remains of architecture at certain sites, have led Israeli archaeologists such as Ram Gophna and Baruch Brandl to conclude that there was an organised, state-sponsored trade network operating under an Egyptian administration at the end of the Protodynastic in 'Dynasty 0'. This conclusion is reinforced by the existence of serekhs incised into sherds from Egyptian pottery jars, eighteen of which have been found in Israel. Most of these are the earlier serekhs surmounted with double falcons, but lacking royal names,

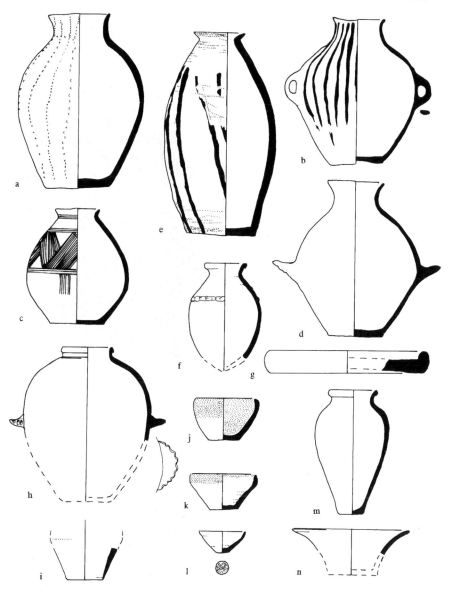

33. (a-d) Imported Canaanite pottery, tomb U-j, Abydos. (After Hartung.) (e) Canaanite hybrid jar, Kafr Ammar. (UC.18271; after Schenck.) (f-n) Egyptian pottery made in local clay, Tell Erani, Israel. (After Brandl.)

34. Part of a Syrian patterned burnished pottery jug with a falcon incised after firing; tomb 1060 of Senar, Tarkhan, time of Djet, First Dynasty. (Courtesy of the Petrie Museum of Egyptian Archaeology, University College London. UC.17089.)

but three are of Narmer, which reinforces the picture of him as a consolidator of influence, although there is no evidence whatsoever of conquest. The large quantity of Canaanite pottery in tomb U-j at Abydos, examples from further south and from Nubia and the Upper Egyptian cultural takeover of Lower Egypt from Naqada IIcd suggest that the administration of the flow of goods was probably in place by early Naqada III. The sites in the east Delta, the north Sinai coast and Canaan were abandoned before the end of the First Dynasty, possibly because improved shipping had made the sea contact with Byblos direct and reduced reliance on the overland trade route with Phoenicia and Syria.

The trade from Canaan in Early Bronze Age I (Naqada II to 'Dynasty 0') is likely to have been chiefly in commodities like wine and oil and there is evidence from content analysis that imported northern Palestinian jars deposited in the First Dynasty tomb of Djer at Abydos were used to contain coniferous resin. Timber, such as pine and cypress, was probably another important commodity, used for the construction of large buildings and ships. One reciprocal commodity from the Nile valley may have been fine linen, and gold was no doubt exported.

Other desirable items required by the growing cultural élite also made their way into Egypt, either from Canaan or through Canaan or by other routes, but the evidence is difficult to assess from the Egyptian side as it concerns the contents of the richest graves and these have usually been plundered. Exotic materials which are not native to Egypt include obsidian, used to produce beads, statue eyes and blades. Although obsidian found in Lower Egypt is suggested to have come from Anatolia, in the south analysis shows that it came from Abyssinia (Ethiopia), probably by the Red Sea coastal trade route, perhaps with Lower Nubia as an intermediary, where obsidian has also been found in A-group cemeteries. Lapis lazuli amulets were found in Gerzean graves at Naqada and in the early Protodynastic tomb 11 at Hierakonpolis and this material is said to be imported from Afghanistan. The fragmentary silver beads which were also found in this tomb are important because as neither native silver nor silver ore occurs in Egypt it was a highly prized material, probably obtained from western Asia.

Gold was part of the wealth of Egypt, but it had to be mined from the eastern desert or brought in from Lower Nubia. Elephantine was an entrepôt for the produce of Africa, where elephant ivory and exotic animal skins would also have entered. Egyptian and Canaanite pottery and Egyptianising artefacts have been found in the Terminal A-group cemeteries of northern Lower Nubia and A-group pottery has been found at sites in Upper Egypt. The Nubian élite grave style with side chamber and accompanying bovid burial which seems to have been copied in the rock-cut tomb 2 at Hierakonpolis is probably of the same date (Naqada IIIa2-IIIb), and not earlier as has been suggested by Bruce Williams. His notion of the existence of a state building centre at Qustul in Nubia and the emergence of a kingdom in Upper Egypt as a result of influences from the south should be absolutely repudiated.

Turquoise and malachite were also mined in the eastern desert, and Anne Bomann surveyed and excavated in the Wadi Abu Had, off the route to the Red Sea from Qena, and discovered an Early Dynastic site where malachite and amethystine quartz were extracted. An expedition to Sinai mounted by king Den of the First Dynasty is mentioned on the Palermo Stone, where it is recorded as a conquest of the land of Sechet, a name later given to western Asia. In Sinai, inscriptions to Hathor, the goddess of foreign countries and 'mistress of the turquoise', were dedicated near the mines in the Third Dynasty.

The Sumerian region was at one time considered the place where the concept of a state and its numerous formative elements originated. The organisation of society, the foundations of economic and religious development, brick architecture and motifs in art and ornamentation, as well as the development of crafts, were regarded as Mesopotamian-

Elamitic achievements transferred and engrafted on Egyptian soil. This exchange of thoughts and ideas was believed to have occurred through the medium of the trade routes leading from Mesopotamia and Elam via Arabia or by sea around the peninsula. Another possible route which may have been used in the mutual, though surely indirect, contacts between Mesopotamia and Elam and Upper Egypt was across the Red Sea and through the Wadi Hammamat to Upper Egypt. A similar course was thought to have been followed by the supposed Asiatic conquerors of Egypt in early Naqada II. The main arguments used in support of this hypothesis were: representations of boats with tall prows and sterns, considered to be Mesopotamian; a sudden appearance of fully developed mud-brick architecture with façades consisting of series of niches and projections (figures 36 and 37); the occurrence in Egypt of typically Asiatic motifs, for instance a hero strangling confronted lions (figure 39), a winged gryphon (figure 35) or cat-like predators with serpentine necks.

35. Decorated ivory fragment with registers of animals in relief including a gryphon, Main Deposit, Hierakonpolis. (Courtesy of the Petrie Museum of Egyptian Archaeology, University College London. UC.14871.)

Kaiser showed in the 1950s that the dating of the boat pictographs in the eastern desert do not corrobate an Asiatic invasion of Egypt and more recent excavations in the Delta leave no doubt that this theory should be finally laid to rest. At the same time, there are still some unquestionable affinities in artistic and architectural themes. It cannot be altogether ruled out that elements of Mesopotamian, and perhaps

36. (Above) The mud-brick niched façade gateway during excavation in 1969, city of Nekhen, Hierakonpolis. (Photograph Michael Hoffman.)

37. (Right) The niched inner wall of the mud-brick Fort at the mouth of the Wadi Abul Suffian at Hierakonpolis. (Photograph Barbara Adams.)

38. The Gebel el-Arak knife-handle. (After G. Bénédite, 'Le couteau de Gebel el-Arak: Étude sur un nouvel objet préhistorique acquis par le musée du Louvre', *Mon Piot* 22, 1916, figure If. Louvre E11517.)

also Elamitic, culture might have penetrated the Delta via Syria and a complex chain of intermediaries somehow passing on architectural concepts.

Some works of art, such as knife-handles from Gebel el-Arak (figure 38) or Gebel Tarif (figure 39), are considered by some investigators to be products of Elamitic craftsmen active in Egypt in the Naqada IIIa phase, whereas others recognise them as the works of imitators. Indisputably there are in Uruk and Susa many stylistic analogies with the motifs present on Egyptian objects – particularly those on Elamite cylinder seals. Nevertheless, the resolution of the problem is impeded by the lack of a well-constructed chronology founded on the latest relevant data which would encompass both Egypt and south-western Asia.

56

There is no doubt that the contacts between Egypt and south-western Asia, mostly of commercial character, with no trace of military conflict, were maintained at least from the middle of the Gerzean. They were intensified in the period of state formation and continued during the first two dynasties. The development of culture in the two territories followed a parallel course, so it is difficult to say if one of these regions exerted a greater influence on the other.

39. The Gebel Tarif knife-handle. (After J. Vandier, *Manuel d'archéologie égyptienne*, Paris, 1952, figure 366. Cairo 14265 and 64737.)

6

Unification and early kings

It is now clear that the processes leading to the emergence of the pharaonic state were the outcome of evolutionary changes and of a gradual expansion of the Naqada culture from the south. The expansion of Upper Egyptian territory was primarily the occupation of new land and secondarily protection for the trade routes leading to Asia. It was also encouraged by the pressure of a greater population in the south, where climatic change in the late Predynastic had reduced winter rainfall and husbandry in the deserts and brought about a reliance on agriculture in natural basins.

The colonisation of the Delta and the rise of the aristocracy were connected in a continuous loop: the conquest of new territories brought about the enrichment of families and individuals as well as the accumulation of property in the hands of the few; bigger élite graves, into which greater quantities of goods were put, stimulated demand for the production of more; and this in turn necessitated the colonisation of further territories and seizure of commercial routes. Egypt moved inexorably towards a national court culture under one king, who strengthened bureaucratic control over Egypt by monopolising the supply of luxury items through trade, controlling their production in royal workshops and dispensing patronage to the nobility. These first nobles (*iry p't*) were members of the royal family, perhaps absorbed into the Thinite house from other regional ruling dynasties, and appear as sandal-bearers or priest-scribes in contemporary representations.

Some would argue that before the addition of the Delta to the valley state there was no 'Egypt' to be united. The expression 'Uniting the Two Lands', introduced retrospectively on the Palermo Stone, did not appear until the reign of Khasekhemwy of the Second Dynasty. Although there are now some linguistic clues, historical interpretations are not agreed and reliance is still placed on models. One suggests that a central authority existed in Upper Egypt from the late Gerzean at Hierakonpolis and that its god, Horus the falcon, became the chief royal deity and the embodiment of kingship. This dominating role is supposed to have been interrupted by the owner of tomb U-j at Abydos, and then the situation was reversed, with the rule of the 'Dynasty 0' of This (Abydos) being interrupted by Scorpion of Hierakonpolis.

According to another theory, three independent proto-kingdoms existed in the late Predynastic period, with their centres at Naqada, This and Hierakonpolis. Naqada declined at the end of the Predynastic and in the

40. The fragments of the Battlefield ceremonial palette. (After W. S. Smith, *A History of Egyptian Sculpture and Painting in the Old Kingdom*, London, 1949, figure 27. British Museum EA20791 and Ash. 1892.1171.)

Protodynastic internal changes and perhaps wars brought about the formation of the Upper Egyptian state with its capital at Hierakonpolis; then the monarchy shifted its burial place to Abydos from the time of Narmer. The annals on the Palermo Stone give the names of seven Predynastic kings of Lower Egypt, most of whom cannot be equated with names known from the archaeological record, and indications by double crown determinatives of another ten kings. Some of the names in serekhs from Lower Egypt are not the same as those from Upper

Egypt, which had led to a convoluted theory of anti-kings or usurpers, but it is more likely to be an indication of the existence of local monarchs and the present paucity of relevant data. Geographically there are eight large mud-brick-lined tombs dating to Naqada IIIb-IIIc between tomb U-j in cemetery U and cemetery B in the Umm el Qa'ab (figure 10), so a historical blank postulated from an artificial lengthening of the chronology is unlikely. The time span involved for the whole of the Protodynastic may have been less than 150 years and there is no need to

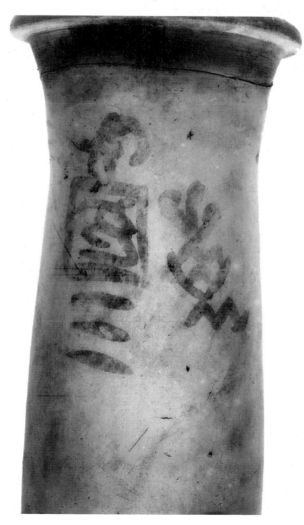

41. Pottery cylinder jar with an ink inscription including a name in a serekh which has been read variously as Ka, Scorpion or Crocodile; tomb 315, Tarkhan. (Courtesy of the Petrie Museum of Egyptian Archaeology, University College London. UC.16071.)

divide it into the reigns of up to ten kings.

Early kings

Petrie's theory of two kings, Iry-Hor and Ka, who are said to have preceded Narmer in 'Dynasty 0', has been resurrected. These 'monarchs' have been assigned the double tombs B1/2 and B7/9 near that of Narmer (B17/18) at Abydos. Alternatively, as the tombs which contain these names also contain the name of Narmer, they could form a complex dated to his reign. Iry-Hor was called Ro by Petrie because the sign on which the falcon stands resembles the r or mouth sign, and he dated him after Ka. The name of Ka does appear in a serekh (figure 21e, i), often with the arms of the sign 'upside down', and the name is known from Lower Egypt, but it is usually associated with descriptions of the produce of Upper Egypt (figure 41). The two titles could be associated with the 'mouth of the king' and the '*ka* (soul) of the king', which would be given equal royal status, symbolising aspects of the monarch's mighty persona and largesse. The pottery types from the grave groups assigned to Iry-Hor and Ka cannot be distinguished from those of Narmer, although the assemblages of Naqada IIIa (U-j at Abydos, tomb 11 at Hierakonpolis and tomb 85 at El Kab) can be separated from IIIb-IIIc. Scorpion is another controversial figure known for certain only at Hierakonpolis, although some people have read his name on inscriptions found in Lower Egypt and Nubia. The names of neither Iry-Hor nor

42. Calcite bowls with incised signs of scorpions and falcons with *ka* signs; Main Deposit, Hierakonpolis. (Courtesy of the Petrie Museum of Egyptian Archaeology, University College London. UC.14954, UC.14953, UC.14951, UC.14952 and UC.14962.)

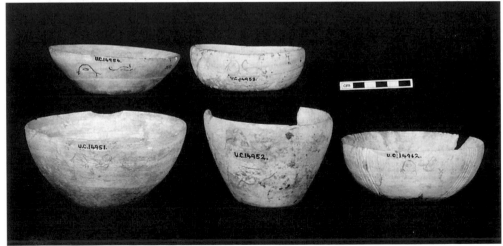

Scorpion ever appear in the royal serekh, although both are found with the falcon and *ka* sign on stone vessels from the Main Deposit at Hierakonpolis (figure 42). If Scorpion, who is depicted in the white crown on the famous mace-head from Nekhen (figure 1), did exist as an Upper Egyptian ruler, he was probably the immediate predecessor of Narmer.

The existence of central rule in Egypt is certain only from the reign of Narmer, the first pharaoh of whom irrefutable traces can be found not only all over Egypt but also far outside it. Whilst he is no longer envisaged as a great conqueror, it is striking that so many monuments bearing his name have been found from Canaan to as far as Nubia, outnumbering those with the names of his immediate successors. Iconographic evidence seems to point to changes occurring in his time: a marked consolidation of the bureaucratic and priestly élite and the development of central administration controlling the entire country.

43. Limestone head of a king, said by Flinders Petrie to be Narmer. (Courtesy of the Petrie Museum of Egyptian Archaeology, University College London. UC.15989.)

Hor-Aha is reckoned to be the first king of the First Dynasty and, according to tradition, he reigned for between thirty and sixty years. His Horus name denotes 'fighting' and he was the first monarch to add the 'Two Ladies' *nebty* name, Men, featuring Nekhbet of Upper Egypt and Wadjet of Lower Egypt, to his royal titulary. This inscription, which is the reason for his identification with Menes by some authors, appears on a label found in a large mastaba for his mother, Neith-hotep, at Naqada (figure 44c). An inscription on another label refers to his expedition to Nubia, and he probably shifted the frontier of Egypt to the First Cataract (Elephantine). He also maintained commercial relations with Canaan and probably with Lebanon. According to Manetho, a temple for the goddess Neith, patroness of the city of Sais, was constructed in his reign and a royal palace was erected in Memphis. His tomb complex at Abydos consists of the double chambers B19, B15, B10 and B13/14 (which contained inscriptions of a possible queen, Benerib), and a double row of subsidiary graves (B16) of slain servants under twenty-five years of age (figure 10). He was the first pharaoh to build a tomb (number 3357) for a high-ranking royal official at Saqqara which had a model estate and a boat grave.

A label depicts a Heb-Sed celebration for Djer in year 30 and Manetho accords him a reign of about forty years. The Palermo Stone records the biennial celebration of a festival confirming the Upper and Lower Egyptian dual character of the Egyptian monarchy in his time. Apart from his expedition to Sinai recorded on the Palermo Stone, his name also appears on a rock inscription at the Second Cataract near Wadi Halfa in Nubia associated with captives and slain enemies below an Egyptian boat. His tomb at Abydos was surrounded by 338 graves for attendants which, with the graves in his funerary enclosure, meant that 580 retainers, mostly women, went to their death with him. A marked development of crafts in his time is evidenced by the finds from the tomb at Abydos and from mastabas 3471 and 2185 at Saqqara, which are dated to his reign.

Djer was succeeded by Djet (Uadji), who is credited with a reign of twenty-three to forty-two years by Manetho, but he is believed not to have ruled more than eleven years, during which he probably continued the policy of his predecessors. His name, engraved on a rock in the Wadi Mijah east of Edfu, may testify to a Red Sea expedition organised during his reign along what was later a well-known caravan route. He had 174 subsidiary burials around his tomb at Abydos and 161 around his funerary enclosure. It seems certain that tomb 3504 at Saqqara was that of his great official Sekhem Ka, whose name is also known at Abydos. The Saqqara tomb is also unique in having three hundred bulls' heads modelled in clay, with real horns, on a low bench around it.

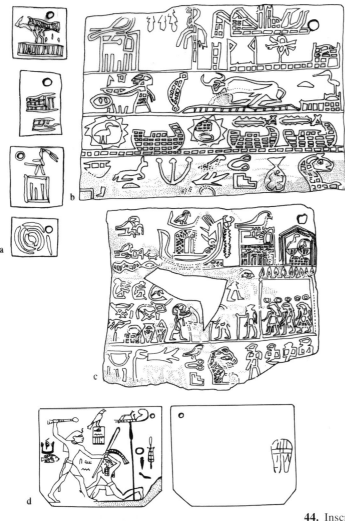

44. Inscribed ivory and wooden labels: (a) tomb U-j, Abydos (after Dreyer); (b) visit to the sanctuary of the goddess Neith, tomb of Hor-Aha, Abydos (Philadelphia E9396); (c) name of Hor-Aha and 'Menes', tomb of Neith-hotep, Naqada (Cairo 14142); (d) Den smiting the east, tomb of Den, Abydos (British Museum EA55586); (e) Heb-Sed jubilee festival of Den (British Museum EA32650).

After Djet's death Merneith, probably his wife and the mother of the heir to the throne, acted as a regent. Her tomb at Abydos attests to the important role played by female members of the royal family. She had forty-one sacrificed servants around her grave at Abydos, whilst tomb 3503 at Saqqara, dated to her reign, also had subsidiary burials containing artisans buried with the tools of their trades.

Den (Udimu) reigned for about forty-five years, but it is possible that Merneith's rule was included in this period. A new royal title appeared, the *nesut-bity* name, meaning 'he who belongs to the sedge and the

45. Stela of the female courtier Kayneith, subsidiary grave 123, tomb of Den, Abydos, First Dynasty. (Courtesy of the Petrie Museum of Egyptian Archaeology, University College London. UC.14273.)

bee', which in his case was Semti (figure 44d). This is usually interpreted as 'the king of Upper and Lower Egypt' and was henceforward an inseparable element of the official protocol with the *nebti* name and the ancient Horus name. The Palermo Stone indicates that he was an energetic king, who undertook numerous expeditions outside the valley against Asians and nomads. This information is reinforced by a label which shows him striking an Asian with the legend 'First time of the striking of the East' (figure 44d). Religious ceremonies were also recorded, such as the consecration of new effigies of deities and his celebration of the Heb-Sed jubilee festival, recorded both by the Palermo Stone and by a contemporary label which represents him during the performance of the ritual running around territorial markers representing the boundaries of Egypt (figure 44e). His tomb at Abydos is among the largest and finest in the necropolis and the first to have a staircase, floored with blocks of granite, descending to the tomb chamber. It was surrounded by the burials of 136 men and women (figure 45), and seventy-seven subsidiary burials have been found around a separate funerary enclosure, originally associated with Merneith. Tomb 3035 at Saqqara, belonging to the chancellor Hemaka, 'ruling in the king's heart', also has a staircase which was blocked with stone portcullises. It is one of three large mastabas at Saqqara and produced the largest collection of archaic objects yet discovered, confirming that the reign of Den was the most prosperous of the First Dynasty. There is also another grave precinct west of the mastaba complex at Saqqara consisting of 231 mostly simple graves in six structured groups around an un-occupied strip. Of these graves, 170 can be dated to the time of Den by similar contents, and they may be associated with a temporary embalming establishment which continued to be used after his reign. The pattern of court and nobility surrounding Egyptian royalty was firmly set for posterity and Den was specially venerated by his immediate successors.

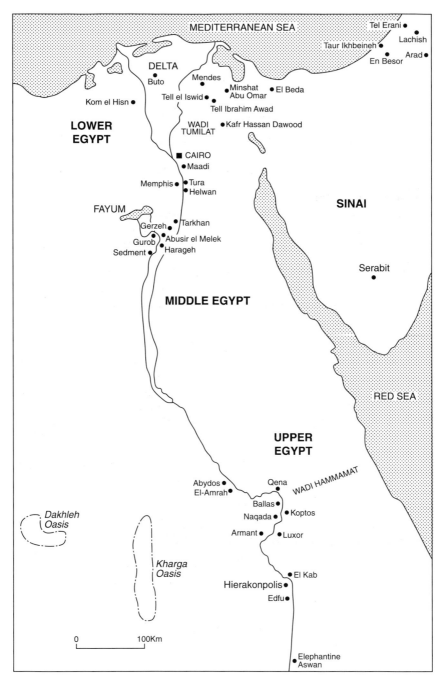

46. Map of Egypt (and Israel) showing sites mentioned in the text.

7

Further reading

Adams, B. *Ancient Hierakonpolis* and *Supplement*. Aris & Phillips, Warminster, 1974.

Adams, B. *Ancient Nekhen: Garstang in the City of Hierakonpolis*. Egyptian Studies Association Publication number 3, SIA Publishing, New Malden, 1995.

van den Brink, E.C.M. (editor). *The Archaeology of the Nile Delta: Problems and Priorities*. Proceedings of the Seminar held in Cairo at the Netherlands Institute of Archaeology and Arabic Studies, 1986. Amsterdam, 1988.

van den Brink, E.C.M. (editor). *The Nile Delta in Transition; 4th-3rd Millennium BC*. Proceedings of the Seminar held in Cairo at the Netherlands Institute of Archaeology and Arabic Studies, 1990. Tel Aviv, 1992.

Emery, W.B. *Archaic Egypt*. Penguin, Harmondsworth, 1961.

Friedman, R., and Adams, B. (editors). *The Followers of Horus: Studies Dedicated to Michael Allen Hoffman 1944-1990*. Egyptian Studies Association Publication number 2, Oxbow Monograph 20, 1992.

Hendrickx, S. *El Kab V: The Naqada III Cemetery*. Publications du Comité des Fouilles Belges en Égypte, Brussels, 1994.

Hoffman, M.A. *Egypt before the Pharaohs*. Routledge, Austin, 1991.

Kemp, B.J. *Ancient Egypt: Anatomy of a Civilization*. Routledge, London, 1989.

Kroeper, K., and Wildung, D. *Minshat Abu Omar. Münchner Ostdelta-Expedition. Vorbericht 1978-1984*. Munich, 1985.

Midant Reynes, B. *Préhistoire de l'Egypte. Des premiers hommes aux premiers pharaons*. Paris, 1992.

Needler, W. *Predynastic and Archaic Egypt in the Brooklyn Museum*. Wilbour Monographs (IX), Brooklyn, 1984.

Payne, J. Crowfoot. *Catalogue of the Predynastic Egyptian Collection in the Ashmolean Museum*. Oxford University Press, 1993.

Spencer, A.J. *Early Egypt*. British Museum Press, 1993.

Spencer, A.J. (editor). *Aspects of Early Egypt*. British Museum Press, 1996.

Vercoutter, J. *L'Egypte et la vallée du Nil*. Tome I: *Des origines à fin de l'ancien Empire*. Paris, 1992.

8

Museums to visit

Museums with Protodynastic objects in their Egyptology collections include the following. Before travelling visitors are advised to check when the museum is open and whether relevant items will be on display.

United Kingdom

Ashmolean Museum of Art and Archaeology, Beaumont Street, Oxford OX1 2PH. Telephone: 01865 278000.

Birmingham Museum and Art Gallery, Chamberlain Square, Birmingham B3 3DH. Telephone: 0121-235 2834.

Bolton Museum and Art Gallery, Le Mans Crescent, Bolton, Lancashire BL1 1SE. Telephone: 01204 522311, extension 2191.

Bristol City Museum and Art Gallery, Queen's Road, Bristol BS8 1RL. Telephone: 0117-922 3571.

British Museum, Great Russell Street, London WC1B 3DG. Telephone: 0171-636 1555.

Castle Museum, Norwich, Norfolk NR1 4JU. Telephone: 01603 223624.

Durham University Oriental Museum, Elvet Hill, Durham DH1 3TH. Telephone: 0191-374 7911.

Fitzwilliam Museum, Trumpington Street, Cambridge CB2 1RB. Telephone: 01223 332900.

Liverpool Museum, William Brown Street, Liverpool L3 8EN. Telephone: 0151-207 0001.

Maidstone Museum and Art Gallery, St Faith's Street, Maidstone, Kent ME14 1LH. Telephone: 01622 754497.

The Manchester Museum, University of Manchester, Oxford Road, Manchester M13 9PL. Telephone: 0161-273 2634.

Museum of Archaeology, Classics and Oriental Studies, University of Liverpool, 14 Abercromby Square, Liverpool L69 3BX. Telephone: 0151-794 2467.

The Petrie Museum of Egyptian Archaeology, University College London, Gower Street, London WC1E 6BT. Telephone: 0171-387 7050, extension 2884.

Royal Museum of Scotland, Chambers Street, Edinburgh EH1 1JF. Telephone: 0131-225 7534.

Sheffield City Museum and Mappin Art Gallery, Weston Park, Sheffield S10 2TP. Telephone: 0114-276 8588.

Swansea Museum, Victoria Road, Swansea, West Glamorgan SA1 1SN.

Telephone: 01792 653763.
Towneley Hall Art Gallery and Museums, Burnley, Lancashire BB11 3RQ. Telephone: 01282 424213.

Australia
Ancient History Teaching Collection, Macquarie University, Sydney, New South Wales 2109.
National Gallery of Victoria, 180 St Kilda Road, Melbourne, Victoria 3004.
Nicholson Museum, University of Sydney, Sydney, New South Wales 2006.

Belgium
Musées Royaux d'Art et d'Histoire, Avenue J.F. Kennedy, 1040 Brussels.

Egypt
Aswan Museum, Island of Elephantine, Aswan.
Egyptian Antiquities Museum, Tahrir Square, Cairo.
Luxor Museum, Luxor.

France
Musée du Louvre, Palais du Louvre, 75003 Paris.

Germany
Ägyptisches Museum, Schlossstrasse 70, 1000 Berlin 19.
Ägyptisches Museum, Staatliche Museen, Bodestrasse 1-3, 102 Berlin.

Italy
Museo Egizio, Palazzo dell' Accademia delle Scienze, Via Accademia delle Scienza 6, Turin.

Sweden
Medelhavsmuseet, Jarntörget 84, Stockholm.

United States of America
The Brooklyn Museum, 188 Eastern Parkway, Brooklyn, New York 11238.
Cleveland Museum of Art, 11150 East Boulevard, Cleveland, Ohio 44106.
Metropolitan Museum of Art, 5th Avenue at 82nd Street, New York 10028.
Museum of Fine Arts, Huntington Avenue, Boston, Massachusetts 02115.
Robert H. Lowie Museum of Anthropology, 103 Kroeber Hall, Uni-

versity of California, Berkeley, California 94720.

University of Chicago Oriental Institute Museum, 1155 East 58th Street, Chicago, Illinois 60637.

University Museum, University of Pennsylvania, 33rd and Spruce Streets, Philadelphia, Pennsylvania 19104.

Index